# WOW!
## IDEAS
### that Changed the World

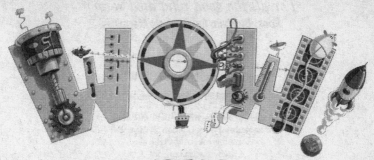

# IDEAS
## that Changed the World

## Philip Ardagh

### Illustrated by Mike Phillips

MACMILLAN CHILDREN'S BOOKS

*For all the good who died young*

First published 2000
by Macmillan Children's Books
a division of Macmillan Publishers Ltd
25 Eccleston Place, London SW1W 9NF
Basingstoke and Oxford
www.macmillan.com

Associated companies throughout the world

ISBN 0 330 48101 0

1 3 5 7 9 8 6 4 2

A CIP catalogue record for this book is available from the British Library.

Printed by Mackays of Chatham plc, Chatham, Kent.

# CONTENTS

# IDEAS!

Imagine a world where no one's come up with the idea of money, so we have to barter for everything – where you were given this book in exchange for a bag of apples or a box of nails. Imagine a world without religions, so there won't have been any Crusades or Inquisitions but there won't have been any spiritual guidance and comfort for billions, either. There are so many things that we accept as everyday parts of our lives that it's easy to forget that they're big ideas put into practice . . . and that, in some cases, people gave their lives to turn these ideas into a reality. In this *WOW!* book we take a look at some of the ideas that changed the way we live or think about the world today. There's the idea that people shouldn't be judged by the colour of their skin. There's the idea that women should have the vote as well as men. There's the idea that everything should be shared equally amongst everyone. And what of the world-changing ideas of the future? Who knows? Perhaps you already have the glimmering of a great idea forming in your mind.

PHILIP ARDAGH
2000

# COMMUNISM

Comrade Vladimir Ilyich Lenin's health is poor and his body weakened – following an attempt to assassinate him some four years earlier – but nothing can take away the feeling of triumph and accomplishment that today brings. Today, after the October Revolution of 1917 and the defeat of the anti-Communist 'White Russians' in 1920, Lenin has lived to see the creation of the Soviet Union – a mighty Communist empire!

## THE IDEA

The *idea* of Communism and how it works in practice are two very different things. The idea of Communism is to be as fair as possible. A Communist society would be a society where all the natural resources – coal, gas, gold and diamonds, for example – belong to the people, along with all the mines and equipment needed to extract them. No one would pay lighting or water bills. All jobs would be shared out equally amongst the people, based on their abilities, and all benefits would be given to people according to their needs. No one would own their own home. Society would build and provide homes for everyone. Once such a society was up and running, there'd be no need for government or rulers, so everyone would be equal. And you can't get much fairer than that.

# THE REALITY

The reality was, of course, very different from the word go, not least because no societies – or very, very few – are built from scratch. In other words, to achieve Communism you need revolution. Because *private* property needs to become *public* property – belonging to all people – it needs to be taken away from the original owners . . . something which most of them are likely to be unhappy about! And such revolutions need to be organized and led and, once the revolution is won, these leaders usually want to keep on leading for fear that, if they don't, others (with different ideas) will. It's all very well saying that everything belongs to everyone and that 'all property is theft', but someone needs to make sure that it stays that way. So there needs to be a police force and an army, and officials to check that the right people are receiving the right benefits and so on and so on. So, in a society where everyone is supposed to be equal, there will still be those with more power and importance than others – and this is why many argue that Communism in *practice* is doomed.

## THE ROOTS OF THE IDEA

The idea of an ideal society being one where the people (the society itself rather than individuals) owned everything and decided everything goes back to Ancient Greece and the writings of people such as Plato. The philosopher Plato (*c.*423BC–347BC) wrote a series

8

of books called the *Republic*, based on the whole matter of justice. This discussed everything from 'what is an individual?' to 'what is the state, or society?'. He saw the ideal state as being made up of three distinct classes: the ruling classes (the wise 'philosopher-kings'), the military classes (the courageous soldiers and sailors) and the merchant classes (the **temperate** traders, creating a healthy economy). What was different about his state, though, was that you weren't born into a particular class. Just because you were the child of a philosopher-king didn't mean that you'd grow up to govern. Just because your dad was a general didn't guarantee you a cushy job in the army. No. Everyone would receive exactly the same education until that person reached a level of education where their ability and interest could take them no further. So the class you belonged to depended on when you stopped your education. Being a philosopher-king required the sharpest mind and the most knowledge so, logically, these would be the pupils who carried on their education right up to the end of the process. For such a republic to work, Plato reasoned, none of the classes must put pressure on any of the others so, as well as wisdom, courage and temperance there had to be justice too. Although the rigid 'three classes' system might not appeal to later Communists, the idea of the same education and opportunities for all most definitely did.

## COMMUNAL LIVING

A number of attempts at creating sharing societies, where people treated each other more equally, came about as a result of religion. These weren't whole countries but small communes (mini-communities) where people lived together on the basis that the good of the commune was more important than the comfort of any one individual. Prime examples of such communes are Christian monasteries, priories and nunneries which spread right across Europe in the Middle Ages. Later, in the sixteenth and seventeenth centuries, when **Protestant** Christians were persecuted, this led to them setting up their own communes – including in places such as America, far away from their persecutors.

## THE NINETEENTH CENTURY

In the nineteenth century a number of cooperative movements flourished, where members benefited from goods and services shared fairly amongst them. However, most members of such groups still lived in mainstream society. One of the most successful experiments in communal living was the Oneida Community, set up in Oneida, New York State in the US in 1848. It'd originally been founded by John Humphrey Noyes in Vermont back in the 1830s, based on the principle that, to be close to God, you must give up all personal possessions and ties – including such things as marriage – and live together in a sharing community. This wasn't too popular with some of the locals, hence the move to New York. A large community, it ran a number of different industries as well as farms and was controlled by a committee. Unusually, women had exactly the same rights as men, and children were raised by the community as a whole. In the end, the original principles of the Oneida Community were lost and, in 1880, the business side of it became a company.

## KARL MARX

True Communism – or at least the theory of it – arrived in the form of *The Communist Manifesto* written by Karl Marx (including ideas of fellow Communist Fredrich Engels) and published in London in 1848. This was a declaration of the aims of a secret group calling themselves the Communist League, founded the year before and made up of German workers and intellectuals who'd been forced into **exile** because of their aims. The introduction contains a warning. 'A spectre is haunting Europe,' it states. 'The spectre of Communism.' Much of the Manifesto discusses the 'class struggle' between what Marx saw as the two main classes: the **capitalists** and the working classes. He called these the 'ruling bourgeoisie' and the 'downtrodden proletariat'. The argument was that the bourgeois capitalists became rich at the expense of the working classes who would eventually rise up against them, and that the Communists would be the true saviours of the working classes. After the inevitable revolution, the working classes would also be the ruling classes – so there would be no such thing as class. The main force behind the Communist Manifesto can best be summed up in its call for action: 'Workers of the world, unite!'

## THE LEGACY OF MARX

The Communist League was disbanded in 1852 and, when Karl Marx died in 1883 – having written a number of other important works, including *Das Kapital* – his mark on the world wasn't that great – but his time would come. It was *after* his death that Marx's words had their greatest influence. His particular branch of Communism became known as Marxism and was the basis of Bolshevism: Marx's theories as developed by the Russian leader Lenin. There were two revolutions in Russia in 1917; in March and in November. The March revolution saw the overthrow of the Tsar (the Russian monarch) and the setting up of a **republic**. The revolution in November saw Lenin and his Bolshevik Communists come to power. (The revolution in November is sometimes referred to as the 'October Revolution' because, at the time, the Russians were using an old calendar system which was thirteen days behind the Western world, putting events in 'their' October.) This second revolution was bloodless. The civil war between the Bolsheviks and anti-Bolsheviks which followed wasn't. Many died on either side, but the Communists were finally victorious. Russia and the soon-to-be-formed Soviet Union was to remain Communist right up until 1991 (see *WOW! Events that Changed the World*).

## CHINESE COMMUNISM

Many people describe the fall of the Soviet Union as the end of Communism, but that's very misleading. China – officially the People's Republic of China – has been governed by a Communist regime since 1949. With 20 per cent of the world's population living in China, this means that, because of that country alone, a lot of people are still living under Communism. The Chinese Communist Party was formed in 1921, in Shanghai, and one of its original members was Mao Tse-Tung. Mao was chairman of the first government council when the Communists came to power and, from 1960 until his death, was chairman of the Communist Party. An incredibly powerful and influential figure, he organized the Cultural Revolution in 1966, during which he published *Quotations of Chairman Mao* (better known as *The Little Red Book*). The idea of this 'revolution' was to achieve pure Communism by force, getting rid of those officials and party members who weren't as true to Communist ideals as it

was thought they should be – with the young betraying the old and the old the young.

## THE USA AND COMMUNISM

Much of the United States' foreign policy over the last hundred years has been concerned with the suppression of Communism. The island of Cuba, lying close to the shores of the US state of Florida, is itself a Communist country, which really annoys a lot of Americans. Whether in Korea, Vietnam or Nicaragua, the US has always supported – either militarily or financially – those fighting a Communist regime or Communist rebels. The importance of the 'space race' (see *WOW! Events that Changed the World*) had as much to do with trying to beat the Communists – in the form of the Soviet Union – to the moon, as the achievement in its own right. In the 1950s, the attempts to weed out Communists in the US itself resulted in the Senator Joseph McCarthy's 'witch hunts' in which hundreds of Americans were accused of being Communists and were **blacklisted**, often simply on the say-so of others. In 1954, McCarthy was finally disgraced into ending what many thought of as a 'paranoid' crusade.

## THE GRIM REALITY

To many older people, the word 'Communism' will always conjure up images of drab streets, a lack of advertising hoardings, food shortages, secret police and people's attempt to escape or **defect** to the West, away from

Communist regimes. They will have memories of the Cold War – between the Communist Soviet Union and the capitalist West – where battles weren't fought with guns but with spies and propaganda. There are those who see little difference between Communist leaders and Fascist dictators, and they may have a point, but this is far removed from Karl Marx's *idea* of Communism: a fairer world for ordinary people.

# PSYCHOANALYSIS

## 23 SEPTEMBER 1939, LONDON, ENGLAND

Sigmund Freud has died. A Jewish Austrian, he fled his homeland the year before, to escape the Nazis, and settled in England. His death makes the world news, as he was one of the greatest and most original thinkers of his generation. His creation of psychoanalysis is a completely new approach to what makes a person's personality, based on the fact that each of us has unconscious as well as conscious thoughts that make us what we are.

## CONSCIOUS THOUGHT

Most of the time we're aware of what we're doing. I'm writing this and you're reading it, for example. Most of the time we know *why* we're doing something – or, at least, we think we do. I'm writing this because I'm an author and I want to share some of these exciting world-changing ideas with you, the reader. You're reading this either because you were told to, because you want to, or because you're bored and you've got nothing better to do. But you probably know – or *think* you know – why you're doing it. Your mind, and therefore *you*, is conscious of why you're doing something.

## THE UNCONSCIOUS

The founder of psychoanalysis, the Austrian Sigmund Freud (1856–1939), argued that we all have a *unconscious* mind as well – that there's a part of our brain that has a big effect on why we do certain things *without our realizing why*. For example, if you had all four books from the *WOW!* series in front of you, and were equally interested in inventions, discoveries, events and ideas, what might have made you pick this one out to look at first? There could be 101 different reasons but they could include the fact that you particularly like the colour of the cover of this book. It could be that this was the same colour as a tricycle you had when you were very little. Now, here's the important part. You don't look at the book and consciously think to yourself: 'the cover of the book is the same colour as the tricycle I had when I was very little. That trike made me feel very happy, so this colour – and in a way this book – does too'. Your conscious mind may simply think 'this book looks nice', whilst *unconsciously*, it's for the reason I've just said.

## IRRATIONAL FEARS

Now apply the same idea of the unconscious mind to more serious matters in a person's life. Some people grow up

17

with what, to other people, seem very strange phobias (irrational fears). There are people who are frightened of birds, spiders, and even buttons. Most of us have at least one such phobia, but it doesn't stop us getting on with our everyday lives. But it's *not* so easy for people with a fear of open spaces, or of confined spaces, or of crossing roads or even talking to other people. If such people could be helped to overcome their fears, then they could lead normal lives. Sigmund Freud argued that, in most cases, the reason why most people have these irrational fears can probably be traced back to an event or situation in the person's past. He suggested that the unconscious mind had a reason – a starting point – for these phobias, usually rooted in early childhood.

## LOOKING FOR ANSWERS

Sigmund Freud then went one stage further and said that, if a person could be made to *remember* this original cause of, for example, the phobia and be made to face it and make sense of it, then he or she could be helped to be cured of it. (As an adult, the person would have more experience and be better equipped to make sense of and understand something which simply upset or frightened him or her as a child.) This is the basis of psychoanalysis.

# THE APPROACH

Psychoanalysis is often described as being an 'analytic therapeutic process', but don't panic! That's a complicated way of saying something more easily explained. 'Analytic' simply means that this is a process of analysing things: examining them very carefully, so as to understand them. 'Therapeutic' means that the process is a part of a treatment. So, as an analytic therapeutic process, psychoanalysis is a way of looking at a person's state of mind, trying to find an explanation as to why things are the way they are, interpret what it means, and then to make changes to 'cure' that person. Unlike many other treatments, however, it is the patients themselves who have to make the changes – with the help of the psychoanalyst – in order to get better.

# THE IMPORTANCE OF DREAMS

Freud also believed that, under the influence of the unconscious mind, rather than a person's thoughts being abstract concepts – such as 'a fear of cheese' – they may be played out like a drama and, in these dramas-in-the-mind, certain objects may be replaced and represented by other objects, or symbols. Unlike in conscious thought, there's no obvious logic to the thoughts and images produced by the unconscious. This, Freud claimed, helped to explain what dreams were – dramas played out in the unconscious mind – and he believed that analysing dreams was a very important part of psychoanalysis.

# ID, EGO AND SUPEREGO

With conscious and unconscious thought at work inside us, Freud and others were keen to try to explain exactly what 'I' means when we talk about ourselves. According to psychoanalysis, there are three constituents of the personality: the id, the ego and the superego.

- The id contains the urges and drives that originally come from our bodies and not our minds – our desire to eat when hungry, for example.
- The ego is what does the thinking, and reacts to the world around us. In an effort for the ego (and us) to function as normally as possible, the ego has a number of defence mechanisms. These include repressing (burying in the unconscious) things it can't cope with right now. (According to psychoanalysis, anxiety is an extremely important emotion because it makes the unconscious mind protect you in many different ways.)
- The superego's job is to modify or hold back any drives or impulses that the id has which might result in a person behaving antisocially – badly towards other people. It's the superego which is supposed to give us our positive image of what we could be: our ideal self.

## FREUD, THE PERSON

Sigmund Freud's most famous work, *The Interpretation of Dreams* was published in 1900 and outlines all the key concepts in his approach to psychoanalysis. It was based on three years of self-analysis in which he wrote down his own dreams and then attempted to analyse them. Five years earlier, he'd published *Studies on Hysteria* with the Viennese

physician Josef Breuer, explaining their work with hysterical patients. In this they describe how patients were hypnotized and 'taken back' to events which had originally caused the **hysteria**, and made to act them out and then sort them out. You can see how this helped lead Freud to his theory of psychoanalysis. Not everyone was convinced by these extraordinary new ideas, however. Although Freud was a qualified physician and **neurologist**, there were many people in the medical profession who thought his 'psychoanalysis' was pure hocus pocus/bunkum, but belief did grow.

## CARL JUNG

One of Freud's earliest and most famous pupils was Carl Jung (pronounced 'Yung'). He later took his approach to psychoanalysis off in a different direction to Freud's, creating what he called 'analytical psychology' (known by some as Jungism). He believed that there were two distinctly different parts to the unconscious mind: the personal unconscious (containing the unconscious memories of the individual) and the collective unconscious (the 'reservoir of the experience of the human race'). He also put forward the belief that there were two different types of personality: introversion and extroversion.

21

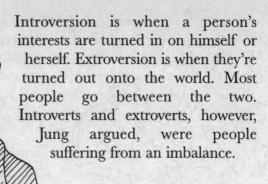

Introversion is when a person's interests are turned in on himself or herself. Extroversion is when they're turned out onto the world. Most people go between the two. Introverts and extroverts, however, Jung argued, were people suffering from an imbalance.

## MORE SCHOOLS OF THOUGHT

Alfred Adler, also a pupil of Freud, went off in yet *another* direction. His belief was that everything anyone does is based on him or her feeling inferior to – less important than – everyone else. Babies feel inferior because they can't feed themselves, Adler argued, and they then grow up trying to be as good as everyone else around them. Fellow student Otto Rank, on the other hand, introduced the idea of neurosis. Since then, many other schools of psychoanalysis and psychiatry have grown up all over the world.

## IT MAKES YOU THINK . . .

Today, there are still many people from all walks of life who believe that Sigmund Freud's ideas were, at the very worst, completely wrong or, at the very best, seriously flawed or misguided. It is undeniable, however – whether one is a believer in psychoanalysis or not – that the development of Freud's theories changed the way we think about the thought process and ourselves, and has led to a healthy debate in trying to understand what it is that makes us what we are.

# ASTROLOGY

## SOMETIME, SOMEWHERE DURING THE SECOND WORLD WAR

It's now or never. Hitler must make his decision. Britain has been the thorn in his side, holding out against V2 rockets fired from the Continent and from bombs dropped from the air. The British Royal Airforce has defeated his own Luftwaffe and, whilst the rest of Europe seems to fall easily into his power, this tiny, pathetic island nation is standing up to the might of the Third Reich! It's time to act! Should he order the invasion of Britain by sea. Surely, yes? But wait – what do the stars predict? The planet alignments are ill-favoured. No! The attack must wait, if it ever comes . . .

## ALL IN THE STARS

Did Hitler really never invade Britain because of astrology? Some say that the story is nonsense. Others say that it's astrology that's nonsense, but it's been with us for thousands of years. Astrology is the idea that the movement and position of planets can actually have control over people on Earth, and that events can be predicted by the studying of them. This shouldn't be confused with astronomy, the scientific study of stars and planets. Today, to *most* people astrology is little more than a bit of fun, looking up your general horoscope in the paper to see what the astrologer says the day has in store for you. In the past, though, astrology could decide the fate of nations.

## HOROSCOPES

A personal horoscope (showing the positions of astronomical bodies at the time of a person's birth) is mapped out inside a special circle called an ecliptic, which represents the path of the Earth's orbit around the sun in a year. This is divided into twelve sections, each named after one of the signs of the zodiac listed on page 26. ('Zodiac' comes from the Ancient Greek *zoidiakos kuklos*, meaning 'circle of animals'.) An astrologer then plots the position of twelve 'heavenly bodies' (ten planets, plus the sun and the moon) within these zodiac signs. Each heavenly body is supposed to represent a specific human drive, and each sign of the zodiac a particular personality type. The zodiac sign in which the sun appears on your chart is called your sun sign. This depends on the day of the year you were born, and people born under particular sun signs, sometimes referred to as 'star signs' (the sun being a star, don't forget), are supposed to have particular characteristics. The ecliptic is further divided into twelve 'houses', with the position of the heavenly bodies within these houses giving revealing information as to a person's health, travel etc.

# SIGNS OF THE ZODIAC
## and 'sun sign' birth dates

Aries (the ram):

21 March-19 April

Taurus (the bull):

20 April-20 May

Gemini (the heavenly twins):

21 May-21 June

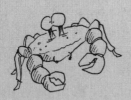

Cancer (the crab):

22 June-22 July

Leo (the lion):

23 July-22nd Aug

Virgo (the maiden):

23 Aug-22 Sept

Libra (the weighing scales):

23 Sept-23 Oct

Scorpio (the scorpion):

24 Oct-21 Nov

Sagittarius, (the archer):

22 Nov-21 Dec

Capricorn (the goat):

22 Dec-19 Jan

Aquarius (the water carrier):

20 Jan-18 Feb

Pisces (the fish):

19 Feb-20 March

# EARLY ASTROLOGY

The idea that the study of the moon, stars and planets might give clues as to the future seems to have been thought of **independently** in different civilizations at different times. Possibly the earliest form of astrology was studied in Babylonia (now southern Iraq) 5,000 years ago in 3000BC. By 1,000 years later – that's 2000BC – the Chinese had their own form of astrology, and then it cropped up everywhere from the Indian continent to the Americas.

## BUT WHY?

We can never know for sure the reason why the movement of planets was seen to be so significant by so many different peoples, but we can have an educated guess. For a start, in the days before automatic lighting inside and out, far more people would have spent time staring up at the night sky, wondering what all those stars were. And, also, people would have come to learn that the success or failure of their crops had to do with how much sunshine they got – and if the sun was responsible for growing crops, who was to say that the moon and planets didn't have other responsibilities of their own? The Babylonians knew about five planets, those which we now call Jupiter, Mars, Mercury, Saturn and Venus. Perhaps because it looked red, and people look red and flushed when they're angry – we even use the phrase 'seeing red' today – they associated Mars with anger, aggression and war.

# ANOTHER 'SCIENCE'

In Ancient Greece, astronomy (the 'proper' scientific study of heavenly bodies) was in existence before astrology, and when astrology reached the Greek shores – in about 500BC – philosophers, such as Pythagoras, simply included it alongside their other sciences. This was also the case in the Middle Ages in Europe. Although the Church was quick to condemn astrology as not fitting in with Christian teaching, it was still taken very seriously right up until the early sixteenth century. It was only when people such as Copernicus and Galileo started understanding why the Earth and the heavens behaved the way they did – with the Earth orbiting the sun and not the other way around – that some of the glamour and magic rubbed off astrology and it became less and less important. (You can read about Galileo in *WOW! Discoveries that Changed the World*.)

# ONE OF MANY GUIDES

In Ancient Roman times, astrologers were just one of many different types of foretellers of the future. As well as astrologers there were 'haruspices', who were priests believed to have a special skill at understanding the insides of sacrificed animals. (For example, the condition of a sacrificed animal's liver was thought to tell a great deal about the Roman gods' attitude towards the government's policies!) Then there were augurs, who 'told the future' by studying cloud shapes or flocks of birds, and the ever-popular fortune tellers who could read your palm or have you throw special fortune-telling dice. But it was usually to the astrologers that the Roman emperors turned, when wanting warnings of possible assassination attempts!

## NOSTRADAMUS

One of the most famous astrologers of all time was the Frenchman Michel de Notredame (1503–66), better known by the Latin version of his name: Nostradamus. He was regularly consulted by the Queen, and later **Dowager** Queen, of France, Catherine de' Medici. In 1555 he wrote a book called *Centuries*, which contained prophecies of events that would happen during the following centuries. Fans of Nostradamus argue that he foretold many events, including the rise to power of Adolf Hitler in Germany in the 1930s and the assassination of US president John F. Kennedy in 1964. Others point out that these predictions – each foretold in four-line rhymes – are so vague and ambiguous that you could make them fit a whole series of events once they'd happened!

# ASTROLOGY TODAY

Today, there are those who genuinely see astrology as an important way of guiding their own lives, and there are those who see it as a multi-million-pound industry. Top newspaper astrologists get paid top money and there are a huge number of books, magazines, CD-ROMs and websites given over to astrology. Some are very serious, some are very colourful and some are plain crazy.

## BELIEVE IT OR NOT

Many people – including me, I confess – don't believe in astrology. They don't look at newspaper horoscopes, and are saddened when otherwise perfectly normal people ask them what star sign they are. To them, it's complete and utter tosh. But that's not the point. The point is that many important people throughout history *did* believe it and astrology did influence *their* decisions and, therefore, major events in world history as well as, eventually, leading to the serious study of astronomy and other sciences. And here's a thought to consider: it's the pull of the moon – a 'heavenly body' – that controls the tides of our seas and oceans on Earth . . . and our bodies are made up of about 70 per cent water, so who's to say that the moon doesn't exert some physical influence on us too? No one can claim to have a definite answer to *that* one.

# MONEY

The cost of shares has been rocketing these past few months, with investors clamouring to buy more, in the hope that their value will go even higher – and then they can sell them at a profit – but now the confidence has gone. The shares are over-valued and in the past few days it's been 'Sell! Sell! Sell!' Today, panic selling is at its worst. Ten billion dollars has been wiped off the value of shares. Thousands of people have lost their investment. Many are left bankrupt, with not a cent to their names. Some will commit suicide.

## A VALUABLE IDEA

Money is an idea which grew. It's an idea which means that something which, in itself, isn't necessarily worth much – a twenty pound note isn't made of twenty pounds' worth of paper, ink and metal strip, if you think about it – now has a totally different value. It's a value not just accepted by the giver and the receiver, but by the whole society using that currency of coins and notes. A fifty pence piece only has value because we've accepted it has that value.

## A LICENCE TO PRINT?

Something that people often ask is, when a country is short of money – say it's at war and needs to buy weapons or food – why doesn't its government simply print more money and spend that? Good question. The answer is that if a government prints more money, left, right and centre, it devalues that currency – in other words, if a twenty pound note is just another printed paper product like a comic or a newspaper, then why should anyone see it as having any more value than a comic or newspaper? People lose confidence in it. That is why countries often used to tie in how much money they had in circulation – in all the banks, tills, purses, wallets, piggy banks, pockets, etc., etc. – with how much gold the government had in their vaults. In other words, for every penny in circulation in a country, there was a penny's worth of government gold. This was called the 'gold standard'. But times change. Today, with international trading of currencies and stocks and shares, it's the strength of a country's **economy**, and a government's control over it (by regulating **interest** rates and spending), that determines the strength or weakness of one country's currency – the value of their money – compared to another.

## THEIR WEIGHT IN GOLD

Of course, there was a time when coins themselves were made of gold and silver, so the amount of money the coin represented was also the genuine value of the coin itself. This is why some old rogues used to 'clip' coins. That is, they trimmed the edges off coins to collect the gold and silver, whilst still being left with a coin with the same face value. ('Face value' is the value we give a coin – what's written on it: 'twenty pence' or 'one pound' for example – rather than its real worth.) To avoid clipping, many coins were given milled edges – little lines all the way around – so it was possible to see if a coin had been clipped. Today, some coins still have milled edges, to make forging harder.

## BARTER, BARTER, BARTER

Before anyone came up with the idea of money, people would barter for goods and services. If you were a fruit grower and you wanted a pair of shoes, you would end up paying for your shoes with fruit, but only if that's what the shoemaker wanted. You might end up paying for the left shoe with fruit and the right shoe by agreeing to help him mend his leaky

roof. There was a lot of give and take on both sides and just because an exchange of goods was agreed one time didn't mean that it would necessarily be agreed again. When fruit was scarce it would be worth more – it would get you more goods in exchange – than when fruit was in plentiful supply.

## ALONG COME COINS

In some societies, rice, dog's teeth, or even figs came to represent a certain value and were used to pay for services, rather than people always having to barter from scratch – so they were a currency of sorts. (In case you were wondering: the rice was in China, the dog's teeth in New Guinea and the figs in Ancient Egypt.) In about 2000BC – 4,000 years ago – it was the Chinese who came up with small bronze tokens in the shape of items used for bartering, including spades and knives, and it could be argued that these were the world's first coins. Numismatists (experts on coins), however, say that this honour actually belongs to the Lydians of Asia Minor, in the seventh century BC (about 2,700 years ago). It was the Lydians who made the first true coins, stamped with an impression on each and each of the same weight. Like all early coins, these had actual as well as face value. They were made from a mixture of gold and silver called 'electrum' but what made them most different from modern coins is that they were shaped more like beans

34

than discs. The first true gold and silver coins were also made and issued in Lydia in the sixth century BC.

## GREAT IDEA

Everyone knows a good idea when they see one, so coins soon caught on and were a big hit in Ancient Greece and Rome. Because the Romans ended up with an enormous empire, ruling much of the (then) known world, their currency spread to numerous countries.

Coins are very useful to archaeologists to help them date sites – a coin under a mosaic floor, for example, can be an important clue as to the earliest time that floor can have been laid.

## HEADS OR TAILS

Most Roman coins included the head of the ruler or emperor on one side, a practice still common in many parts of the world today. In Britain, coins have long had a head of the ruling **monarch** on one side and another image on the other. The correct term for the side of a coin with the head on it is the 'obverse' side, whilst the other side is called the 'reverse'. When flipping a coin, though, they're more commonly known as 'heads' and 'tails'. 'Tails' probably comes from the fact that the head is the top of your body and the extreme opposite of that would be the tip of your tail – if you had one! During the rule of the Commonwealth in Britain, under the Lord Protector Cromwell in the seventeenth century, however, coins didn't have heads on them. (Neither did King Charles I – he'd had his chopped off now that Cromwell's lot were in power.) So which was 'heads' and which was 'tails' on a Commonwealth coin would be very difficult for us non-experts to guess!

## A LASTING IMPRESSION

It was very important that only monarchs, emperors or governments issued coins, so that control could be kept on their value and people accepted their worth. Right up until 1500, coins in the Western world would have been hand-struck: the metal impression of heads and tails stamped by hand. It was the Italians who produced the first uniformly shaped and stamped coins. (Before then, coins were never terribly round, and the stamping was often off-centre and not too well done!) Now the Italians created a system of punching out perfectly round discs which were then stamped in special screw-down presses. All British coins were now made under strict control by the Royal Mint.

## PAPER MONEY

The idea for paper money, or banknotes (what Americans call 'bills'), was probably invented by the very brainy Chinese. They were certainly using them in AD800 – that's about 1,200 years ago. According to tradition, they came about to prevent theft. When members of the Imperial Court were regularly bringing bags of money to the emperor, their horses were weighed down with all the coins so were easy targets for bandits lying in wait. They couldn't gallop away from an ambush. Paper money solved that. It was as light as – as paper, and soon gained the nickname 'flying money'. Not only could people carrying paper money easily gallop away at high speed at the first sign of trouble, but it was also difficult for bandits to tell who was carrying money and who wasn't!

## TYPES OF MONEY

There are, in fact, three main types of money. I don't mean different currencies. There are plenty of them, from individual countries' currencies – pounds, dollars, lira, roubles – to a shared common currencies, such as the Euro, but I'm talking about types of money in terms of how it's valued. We've discussed them already, but here's how they're divided up and what they're called.

- The first type is when the face value of a coin is the same as its actual value. (So the face value of a gold coin, say, is literally worth its weight in gold.) This is called 'commodity money', because the coin itself is a commodity. It has value.
- The second type of money is called 'credit money'. That's what banknotes are. If you look at a British banknote, you'll find that it has 'I promise to pay the

bearer on demand the sum of . . .' on it. In theory, the idea is that, if you were to go to the Bank of England in London and give them a note, they'd have to change it into coins for you. But please don't try it or, if you do, please don't mention my name. I said *in theory*. In practice, that may be how the system works, but there are easier ways of getting change. It's simply that, for example, one million pounds' worth of £50 notes are far cheaper and easier to transport than one million pounds in pound coins or twenty pence pieces, so credit notes – banknotes representing that amount of coinage – are issued.

- The third main type of money has the strangest name. This is 'fiat money', and it has nothing to do with cars. Fiat money is simply money that has the face value it has because the government that issued it says so. So there. Most coins are fiat money. A penny isn't commodity money because it isn't actually worth a penny in itself, and it isn't credit money because even the Bank of England – in theory or practice – can't change it into anything smaller for you. It's worth a penny because the government says so. And that's that.

## A MONEYLESS CURRENCY

Today the idea of money is as important as it's always been. We still expect to pay for things and to be paid. The big difference is that banks, building societies, shops and businesses are doing their best to encourage us not to use actual money. We can pay for things by cheque or credit card or debit card. More and more people's salaries and benefits are paid directly into their accounts – which is really the transferring of figures onto one record from another, not actually someone popping around with bags of cash. This means that we can buy things over the phone or via the internet – we don't have to see the buyer or seller face-to-face. The original idea of money completely changed the way we live and do business. Now we're probably about to enter a whole new phase in the way it actually changes hands. In the not too distant future there may be no actual money – no coins or notes – at all.

# WORLD RELIGIONS

## MARCH 2000, JERUSALEM, THE DIVIDED CITY

Looking old, and frail with illness, Pope John Paul II, leader of the Roman Catholic Church, is in this ancient city, sacred to Jews and Christians alike. It is here, in front of an audience of Jews and Muslims, that he makes a historic apology for the death and destruction caused to Muslims and Jews by Christians during the bloody Crusades – the 200-year religious wars of the Holy Land, fought on this very soil.

## POWERFUL BELIEFS

The ideas which have probably had more influence than any others in the world's history are the ideas set out in the teachings of the world's various religions. That's why you'll find that this is the biggest chapter in all four books of the *WOW!* series. On a basic level, religion is a belief in a supernatural power (or powers) that created or rules over the universe, including people's destiny – in other words, a general belief in a god or gods. More specifically, it's an institutionalized system of expressing that belief – different organized religions (as institutions), such as Hinduism,

Judaism and Christianity, have different beliefs and different ritual ways of observing such beliefs.

## PERSONAL AND SHARED

The actual word 'religion' comes from the Latin word '*religio*'. Latin was the language of the Ancient Romans (see *WOW! Events that Changed the World*) who 'stole' most of their gods and goddesses from the beliefs of the Ancient Greeks, simply changing their names. The Roman king of the gods, Jupiter, for example, was the Greek king of the gods, Zeus!

'*Religio*' means the observing of ritual duties and also having a deep, inner belief, which neatly sums up the requirements of most major religions: to believe and follow a code of practice (a way of behaving) is not enough. You must express your belief by following the particular rituals of your particular faith, whether it be praying at certain times throughout the day, going through certain rights at certain ages – such as the Jewish *bar mitzvah* – or simply attending religious services.

# MYTHS AND LEGENDS

What some people might see as a country's myths and legends –'traditional tales' – others might see as a part of their religious beliefs. Myths are said to be traditional stories that are based on events that didn't really happen, often containing super-humans, and that were told to help explain local customs or natural phenomena (such as why it rains, or what lightning is). Legends are slightly different in that they might be based on people who really lived, or events that really happened, which have been changed and built up into something bigger and more dramatic over time. But you have to be careful. What you think of as 'a good story' may, to someone of a certain faith, be seen as an important part in the history or teaching of their religion. They may be sacred stories or even part of their scriptures.

## COMMON STORIES

Most countries have creation myths (explaining how the world came into being) and these are included in the sacred writings of many religions. This is hardly surprising. Most religions have a god as the creator of the Earth, so they need to explain exactly how that god did it. Another common theme is a terrible flood sent by a god to punish humans. The story of Noah and the Ark, filled with animals, is familiar to Jews and Christians. Ancient Greeks would have been familiar with the story of the son of the god Prometheus building a boat and surviving with his wife. Hindus are familiar with the story of Matsya the fish – actually the first **incarnation** of the god Vishnu –

warning the first human, Manu, to build a boat and fill it with 'the seed of all things'. There are similar ancient flood stories from Australia, Babylonia, China and South America, to name a few. These are a part of the sacred histories of the different faiths.

## KEY EVENTS

Each of the world's main religions has a sacred history based around the key event (the most important moment) in that particular faith. In Judaism – the Jewish faith – the part most central to its teaching is the Jews' flight from slavery in Egypt (the Exodus) and Moses receiving the Ten Commandments from God. Although Christians also believe in these events, which are contained in the  Old Testament of their Bible, the key event in their sacred history is God's coming to Earth in the form of Jesus Christ, his teachings, his crucifixion and resurrection (coming back to life). For Muslims (followers of Islam), the most important moment was when Allah (God) gave divine revelations to the prophet Mohammed, which were written down and put together to form the *Koran*. Buddhists see Buddha's moment of enlightenment as the central part of their sacred history and teachings.

# A PLACE IN THE WORLD

There are some people who have no religious beliefs. They don't believe that there are any gods or deities, or that there is any life after death – whether it be as a soul in heaven or as a part of **reincarnation** (coming back as another person or animal) – a common belief in many religions. A common argument of 'non-believers' is that the various religions have grown up to feed a certain human need. In other words, if the gods aren't true, humans would have made them up anyway! Early humans will, for example, have worshipped the sun because it brought them heat and light and helped the crops grow – and they wanted to keep on the right side of it, so that it stayed friendly and came back every morning. By creating gods, they suggest, humans gained a sense of safety and belonging and, over the centuries, specific ideas and rituals have grown up around these beliefs.

## WITHOUT SENDING A SIGN

Being religious is often referred to as 'having faith' and religions are sometimes called 'faiths'. This has come about because the word 'faith' means having the confidence and belief in an idea or person without necessarily having proof. In other words, religious people don't actually have to have met their god or gods face-to-face in order to believe in their existence.

## TYPES OF RELIGION

Over the years, experts have tried to divide faiths into different categories. Some suggest that the earliest beliefs were probably in spirits – people thinking that most, if not all, objects from trees to water to rocks had spirits inside them. ('If I have thoughts and feelings, then why can't a tree?') This type of belief has been labelled *animism*. This then developed into a belief that there were a variety of gods controlling their lives – the sun god, the moon god, the thunder god and so on – which is called *polytheism* (*poly* means 'many'). Later, these experts reasoned, this was refined into the idea of one single god, which is called monotheism (*mono* means 'single'). But, as is true with experts in just about every subject, not all of them agree with this! Some argue that religion probably began as worshipping nature, developed into worshipping their dead ancestors and then into trying to overcome the fear of death by believing in reincarnation or the afterlife. Either approach is based on the theory that religion developed out of people trying to make sense of the world around them. If you understand something, then it becomes less frightening.

## 'CHURCH' AND STATE

In the past, religion was central to official life in most countries (and still is in many countries today). In most cases it was impossible to divide official religion and the state. Religion affected everything from architecture, education, painting and writing, to the clothes people wore . . . even the calendar. All the dates in this book are either BC, 'Before Christ', or AD, '*Anno Domini*', meaning 'Year of Our Lord' – the birth of Jesus being the starting point for the calendar now used by much of the world. (The Islamic calendar begins in what the Western world generally calls AD622. The Jewish calendar begins way, way back in what Christians call 3760BC.)

## FROM THE CRADLE TO THE GRAVE

Even in Britain, where only a very small percentage of people regularly attend church, the trappings of religion – the rituals – are often used to mark important moments in people's lives. Couples who never go to church otherwise often want to get *married* in a church, or have their children christened (**baptized** with holy water). Again, the same can be said about death. Most British people who aren't practising Christians (but are not, of course, believers in another faith) choose to have Christian funeral services and burials – which is as much a part of the nation's culture as it is to do with any actual heartfelt beliefs.

## RITES OF PASSAGE

To believers, however, these rites of passage – rituals marking significant points in their religious and personal lives – are an extremely important part of expressing their faith, and different religions have different ceremonies at different times. In addition to birth, marriage and death ceremonies, for example, entry into 'adulthood' is marked by ceremonies called *bar mitzvahs* and *bat mitzvahs* for thirteen-year-olds of the Jewish faith. Christians take their First Holy Communion or are confirmed. Many other faiths have their own rituals to mark such occasions.

## HIGH DAYS AND HOLY DAYS

Most religions require followers to spend a certain amount of time celebrating and thinking about their faith. For **devout** Muslims, this means praying five times a day. For Christians, this may simply mean attending a service in a church once a week. Then there are dates in the various religious calendars that are of special significance and which require special rituals: Christmas and Easter are important times for Christians, Yom Kippur and Passover are important to Jews, and Ramadan is important for Muslims – with a whole month of **fasting** during daylight hours.

## RELIGIOUS WARS

Because the teachings of many faiths are concerned with people getting along peacefully together, many people of different faiths live happily side by side. There are, however, still religion-based conflicts in the world today and, in the past, there were regular religious wars. This is one reason why the idea of religion, or religious ideas, have had such a huge impact on the world we live in today. Over the centuries, millions of people have died for their religious beliefs: Christians and Jews in the Roman arena, Muslims at the hands of Christians during the Crusades, Christians at the hands of fellow Christians during the

Spanish Inquisition, and Jews at the hands of the Nazis during the Holocaust in the Second World War. The list is very long and very bloody.

## THE ARENA

A popular spectator sport back in Ancient Rome was a day at the amphitheatre watching 'the games'. An amphitheatre was a huge, round, open-air building with an arena in the centre where the actual games took place. There was a whole variety of games, but they all had one thing in common: they were violent and often very bloody. There were gladiator fights. There were fights between wild animals – and there was a real crowd-pleaser which involved unarmed 'criminals' being thrown to the lions (or other, equally vicious) wild animals. These 'criminals' were often Christians or Jews because they regularly refused to give up their own God to worship Roman gods instead. Eventually, Rome ended up with its own Christian emperor, and this activity was stopped! (See *Wow! Events that Changed the World*.)

## THE CRUSADES

The Crusades were the wars fought between West European Christians and Muslim from 1096 to 1291. The Christians wanted to recover the Holy Lands – what is now Israel and Israeli-occupied territory – from the Seljuk Turkish Muslims. The First Crusade aimed to recapture the city of Jerusalem, which was sacred to Christians. They succeeded in 1099, killing many Muslim (and Jewish) people living there, and ruling very harshly. Hence the modern-day Pope's apology. The Muslim leader Saladin managed to recapture Jerusalem in 1187, and the aim of the Third Crusade by the Christians was to get it back *again*. Led by King Richard the Lionheart of England and King Philip of France, they failed. There were eight Crusades in all, and they were probably as much to do with Europe flexing its military muscle to try to gain territory as to do with true Christian beliefs.

## INQUISITIONS

In the thirteenth century, the 'official' Christian religion was the Roman Catholic Church, with the Pope at its head as 'God's representative on Earth'. The Church had extraordinary power and influence over the countries of Western Europe, in some instances owning as much land in a country as its monarch. Kings and queens may have ruled their own nations, but most went out of their way to stay in the Church's good books. Anyone disagreeing with the Church's statements or rulings on matters were called heretics, and what they said in disagreement was called heresy. In 1231, Pope Gregory XI (the 'XI' just means he was the eleventh pope with that name) ordered his Inquisitors to interrogate those suspected of heresy and to persecute heretics. It generally only took two alleged witnesses for a suspect to be found guilty, and there were many accusations. It was the Spanish Inquisition, which began in 1478, that resulted in the greater horrors and miscarriages of justice. Set up to weed out Jewish and Muslims who'd been forced to become Christians because of cultural pressures, it later turned into the persecution of Protestants (any Christians who'd broken away from the teachings of the Roman Catholic Church). Many thousands of so-called heretics were executed. Spanish monk and grand inquisitor Tomás de Torquemada alone ordered about 2,000 people to be burnt at the stake, and the torturing of many more.

## THE HOLOCAUST

The Holocaust, when spelled with a capital 'H' (and also known as the Shoah), was the mass murder of Jewish people living in continental Europe during the Second World War (1939–45). It was a part of the Nazi dictator Adolf Hitler's plan to wipe out the Jewish race. Jewish people were rounded up and kept in ghettos before being piled into cattle trucks and taken to death camps in Poland, the most infamous of which was Auschwitz. It is estimated that approximately six million Jews died. The word 'holocaust' comes from the Latin '*holocaustum*' which means 'whole burnt offering'.

## A WORLD OF RELIGIONS

There are, of course, a vast number of different religions and beliefs across the globe. Native North Americans, those people living in the South American rainforests, the most isolated tribespeople in Africa – to name just a few – have beliefs as important to them as Islam is to a Muslim or Christianity to a Christian. It's what you individually believe that is important. There are, however, a number of religions whose followers make up the majority of religious people in the world. In alphabetical order, they are: Buddhism, Christianity, Hinduism, Islam (the Muslim faith), Judaism (the Jewish faith) and Sikhism, and I thought it'd be a jolly sensible idea to end this chapter with a quick outline of each. So here you have it, the *WOW!* whirlwind guide to world religions . . .

## BUDDHISM

Buddhism grew up in the sixth and seventh centuries BC in eastern North India, where Hinduism was the main religion. It's based on the teaching of Siddhartha Gautama, who became the Buddha, or 'Enlightened One'. Buddhism rejects the **Vedic** scriptures and is founded on the search for release from the endless cycle of reincarnation humans are subjected to. It believes that a person can ultimately escape being born again and again by achieving

Enlightenment. There are two main branches of Buddhism, Theravada and Mahayana, and it is practised in a great many countries, having anything up to 300 million followers.

## CHRISTIANITY

Christianity is the most widely spread religion in the world, with around 1.7 billion followers – that's 1.7 thousand million Christians. Christianity is based around the life and teachings of Jesus Christ. According to Christians, Jesus was the son of the one God, who appeared in human form, and who died on the cross to give people the chance to be forgiven their sins if they followed his teachings. He is said to have risen from the dead and ascended to Heaven. Christians believe in an afterlife. The Christian scriptures, the Bible, is divided into the Old Testament (containing events before Christ's birth, which form a part of the Jewish faith) and the New Testament (starting with his birth).

# HINDUISM

The main religion in India, Hinduism, was founded in 1500BC and has an estimated 700 million followers. Tribes of people, called Aryans, first settled in India in 2550BC. Over time, they settled the whole subcontinent and became known as the Hindus, which means 'of the Indus' (after the Indus valley). The Aryans' cycle of stories and teachings, passed down the centuries by word of mouth, were finally recorded in four separate collections. These became the basis for the Vedic religion. Between *c*.900 and *c*.500BC this, in turn, developed into a new religion including new Hindu gods and goddesses. (Vedic gods were still there, but playing more minor roles.) Central to the beliefs of Hinduism is reincarnation and the most important Hindu sacred texts are the *Puranas*.

# ISLAM

Based on the teachings of the Prophet Mohammed, 'Islam', according to its sacred book the *Koran*, means 'to surrender to God's will'. Followers of Islam, called Muslims, believe in one God who has four main functions: creation, **sustenance**, guidance and judgement. In

return, it is the duty of human beings to give their lives to the service of God and to try to lead as pure a life and to create as pure a society as possible. On the Day of Judgement the good will go to Heaven and the failures to Hell. God, however, is forgiving and will look upon the deserving with kindness. There are over one billion (one thousand million) Muslims in the world today.

## JUDAISM

Judaism – the Jewish faith – began in Israel and the surrounding lands, and the modern state of Israel offers citizenship to all Jews. There are between 12 million and 13 million Jews worldwide, and they believe in one God who continues to govern the universe. According to Judaism, God revealed his instructions to the Jews and these revelations are recorded in the sacred writings of the *Torah*, his commandments. A covenant – agreement – was made between

God and the Jews, his chosen people. The *Torah* forms part of their sacred book, the *Tanach* (sometimes called the Jewish bible and containing the same material as the Christian Old Testament), the other two sections being the *Pentateuch Nebiim* ('the prophetic literature') and the *Ketubim* ('the other writings'). A second book, called the *Talmud*, contains discussions and commentaries on the first, as well as laying down Jewish religious law. Jews are waiting for the coming of a Messiah whose arrival can be hastened by the study of the scriptures.

## SIKHISM

Sikhism, the most recent of all the religions outlined in this chapter, was founded by Guru Nanak (1469–1539). Born a Hindu, he travelled with a Muslim on a pilgrimage of enlightenment, settling in the Punjabi region of India in 1520. He soon earned a reputation as a wise teacher and many came to learn from him. He taught the Unity of God and the Brotherhood of Man. His followers became known as Sikhs, which means 'learners'. After his death, there were a series of gurus, the final – Guru Gobind Singh – dying in 1708. Since then, the religion has had no spiritual leader. All guidance comes from reading their holy book the *Adi Granth*, itself called a guru and renamed the *Guru Granth Sahib*. Sikhism has over 20 million followers.

# DARWINISM

## 12 FEBRUARY 1809, SHREWSBURY, SHROPSHIRE, ENGLAND

Almost six years have passed since the death of Josiah Wedgewood, one of the most famous British potters whose name and fine pottery will live on for many generations. Sadly, he is not alive to witness the birth of his daughter's fifth child, today. The baby – a boy – Charles Robert, will not only one day grow up to become even more famous than him, but his ideas will actually change the way that most of us see the living world around us – because this tiny baby grandson is Charles Darwin.

## OUT OF THE ORDINARY

Darwinism gets its name from the British scientist Charles Darwin (1809–82). Today, most scientists and ordinary people – with the noticeable exception of Creationists, who take the story of **Genesis** to be the absolute truth – take the theories put forward in Darwin's books *On the Origin of the Species by Means of Natural Selection* and *Descent of Man* to be fact. His is the generally accepted view of how animals and humans evolved, and those who think otherwise are the ones who are often seen as the 'odd ones out'. However, that certainly wasn't the case when he first published his ideas.

## MEET THE ANCESTORS

Before we go any further, it's important to dispel a few common **misconceptions** about Darwinism. Many people believe that Charles Darwin wrote a book called *The Origin of the Species*, that the 'species' referred to were humans, and that in it he stated the belief that human beings are descended from apes. The truth be told, *The Origin of the Species* is a shortening of the full title of the 1859 book *On the Origin of the Species by Means of Natural Selection* (the '*On*' was dropped when the third edition was published). The 'species' referred to are *all* species of plant and animals, not just humans, and he never wrote *anywhere* that he believed that humans are descended from apes. What he did say was that humans and apes probably had

a common ancestor. This is a big difference because, if we were descended from apes, what's stopping existing apes, such as those in London Zoo, evolving – developing over generations – into humans? This is clearly ridiculous. If, however, both apes and humans are descended from a common ancestor which died out millions of years ago – and there are far more similarities between humans and monkeys than there are differences, as modern DNA testing has shown – then there's no danger of that happening!

## NATURAL SELECTION

The most important part of Darwinism, however, appears in the words at the end of the title of his book: *Natural Selection*. It was Charles Darwin's belief that the animals that are on the Earth today are the animals who have adapted best to survival. Take an imaginary example: a species of creatures – let's call them snuffles – survive by eating berries growing on a particular type of bush. They are small creatures so can only reach and eat the berries growing on the branches near the bottom of the bush. The more snuffles there are, the more berries get eaten off the lower branches and, because there aren't enough berries to go around on those bottom branches, some snuffles die. Like people, snuffles come in different shapes and sizes, so some snuffles have longer legs than others. Because longer legs mean that they can reach higher up the bush, they can get to eat more berries long after the lower branches have been stripped bare. So the long-legged snuffles survive and breed, eventually creating more long-legged snuffles, until *all* snuffles look that way – and those which were originally seen as 'normal' snuffles die out. Nature has seen to the survival of the fittest – not necessarily fittest as in healthiest but as in best adapted to suit the world around them – but it's important to remember that such changes occurred over very long periods of time.

## AN IMPERFECT WORLD

The reason why this idea was so unpopular with Christians at the time – and Britain saw itself as a very Christian nation – is obvious. The Bible states that God created Adam and Eve and the animals as they are now. Darwinism states that they evolved, with the less well-adapted members of a species (and sometimes even whole species) dying out along the way. To accept Darwin's views would not only be to accept that the Bible was wrong, but also to accept that God made imperfect creatures, which couldn't adapt as well as others.

## THE FOSSIL PROBLEM

The problem with backing up this widely accepted Christian view was fossils. These showed the remains of incredible creatures that weren't around any more. What were they then? These were explained by the catastrophists' theory – the idea that the Earth had been subjected to dramatic, violent changes, following natural catastrophes, the most recent of which had been the flood for which, according to the Bible, Noah built his ark. Each set of animals would have been wiped out in these disasters, and the animals on the Earth today must obviously be descended from those saved by Noah. Plain and simple.

## THE AGE OF THE EARTH

Then there was the commonly held belief in Britain in the late eighteenth and early nineteenth centuries that the Earth could only be about 4,000 years old. This figure was, again, reached from information contained in the Bible, by linking people from generation to generation all the way back to Adam and Eve and the creation story. In 1785, however, a Scottish geologist called James Hutton argued that, by looking at the geological processes going on around him – the speed at which rivers wore away riverbeds or rain eroded rocks – it would have taken the world millions, not thousands, of years to end up in the condition it had then reached – and, slowly but surely, the scientific world began to listen. But rocks and soil were one thing, animals and people were quite another.

## THE VOYAGE OF *THE BEAGLE*

Charles Darwin was a naturalist onboard a ship called *The Beagle* which, from 1831 to 1836, was on a voyage to survey the **southern hemisphere**, making accurate maps and records of the flora (plants) and fauna (animals) to be found in these faraway places. He started out the journey aged just twenty-two and, although he was unpaid, this was an incredible opportunity for a brilliant young mind. It was when he reached the Galapagos Islands that he made a most interesting discovery . . .

## EACH TO THEIR OWN

Here was a group of islands with similar tortoises and birds on each island. But they were only similar. They were *not* the same. There were significant differences between the tortoises on each island, and it was the same with the mocking birds and finches too. They were different varieties. Now, if God had placed them there, surely they'd all be the same? Then Darwin noticed that the habitat for these creatures – the environment the animals survived in on each island – differed slightly on each island too. An idea was already forming in Darwin's mind: the tortoises and birds on each island had to adapt to fit in best with the environment of their particular island. On returning to England in 1836, he spent many years and filled many notebooks trying to make sense of the information he'd gathered. (It may seem obvious to us now, but that's because he did all the work for us!)

## THE NEWS BREAKS

Darwin first shared his theories with the world when he read out a scientific paper in 1858. This was the same year that another brilliant naturalist Alfred Russell Wallace announced a similar theory, which he'd come up with quite independently of Darwin. It was the publication of Darwin's *On the Origin of the Species by Means of Natural Selection*, a year later, that really caused the sensation. All copies were sold on the very first day of publication and it quickly went through six further editions.

## NO PROOF!

Darwin's ideas weren't only attacked by the Church but also by many fellow scientists. They argued that he couldn't *prove* them, which was true enough. People couldn't simply sit around and wait to see if animals evolved around them – evolution was a slow process! Then, they argued, how could animals with particularly useful characteristics – for example, the snuffles with the longer legs, in my made-up example on page 58 – so conveniently pass these characteristics onto their offspring? That couldn't be explained either. Not in those days, maybe, but with today's understanding of genetics (which you can read about in *WOW! Discoveries that Changed the World*), we know that Darwin was right. Such characteristics can be passed on through **genes**.

## THE LAST STRAW

What angered the Christian Church most of all, though, was Darwin's theory of 'common ancestry' and the way that he grouped human beings together with other animals. Surely the creation of human beings, at least, must have been special, and separate from that of all other creatures? Again, today we have the advantage of modern science to support Darwinism. We now know that the first true humans, *homo sapiens sapiens* – which is what we are – first walked on this Earth about 100,000 (not 4,000) years ago and that we shared the planet with a group of 'almost humans' – *Homo sapiens neanderthalensis* who died out about 30,000 years ago. They probably weren't as well suited to the environment as the bigger-brained *homo sapiens sapiens*.

## THE DESCENT OF MAN

*On the Origin of the Species by Means of Natural Selection* has been described as 'the book that shook the world' because, in the end, it altered so many people's way of thinking about the world around them. Then, in 1871, Darwin produced his second best-known work: *The Descent of Man*. In this instance 'descent' doesn't mean the 'decline' or 'fall' of humans – Man was short for humankind, both men and women – but 'descent' as in 'descendants and ancestors', in other words: the **lineage** of the human race.

 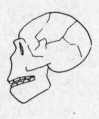 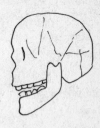

| 3–2 MILLION YEARS AGO | 750,000 YEARS AGO | 100,000 YEARS AGO TO PRESENT |

# THE LEGACY

Today, Darwinism is taken for granted by so many that it's difficult to imagine that it's actually a group of ideas put together and argued by one man. Later in his life, Charles Darwin himself became more accepted by society in general. Today there are many scientists who are happily Christian (though not Creationists) *and* believers in Darwinism too. Charles Darwin is buried in Westminster Abbey, which was not only a great honour but also a place of Christian burial.

# VOTES FOR WOMEN

## 4 JUNE 1913, EPSOM DOWNS RACECOURSE, ENGLAND

As the king's horse thunders around the bend in the racecourse a woman ducks under the railings and steps right into its path. What on earth's going on? What's she doing? Trying to attract attention? Make some kind of protest – or is she on a suicide mission? The crowd looks on in horror as the woman is trampled underfoot, toppling horse and jockey. She is – she was – Emily Davidson, a suffragette, fighting for the idea of votes for women. Whatever her original plan, she has just given her life for that cause. A riot will break out and over 6,000 will attend her funeral.

## FAIR'S FAIR

The idea that a person can't vote in any kind of government election or referendum simply because she's a woman may seem incredible to you. That's probably because we now live in a society where everyone over eighteen who's registered – and isn't 'of unsound mind' or a prisoner serving a sentence – has that right, but it was a hard-fought one. Countries which have been held up as shining examples of **democracy**, such as Ancient Greece and Rome, were only democratic compared to other countries, because even there the men certainly didn't allow the women to elect any representatives.

# KEEP WOMEN SPECIAL

That's not to say that all women thought that they should be given that right. When the idea of 'votes for women' was at its height at the end of the nineteenth and beginning of the twentieth century, there were those women who argued that it was far better for women to influence men rather than actually getting involved in the mechanics of elections. They saw women as having a unique, special and different contribution to make to society, and voting would destroy this. They were known as the 'antis' which was short for the 'anti-suffragists'. The suffragists, on the other hand, were people who believed in equal voting rights for women. The name comes from the word 'suffrage' which – far from being about pain and suffering – actually means 'the right to vote'.

# ALL WALKS OF LIFE

There's a general misconception that the suffragists in Britain were all nice 'middle-class' ladies from comfortable backgrounds. However, by the 1870s, more and more 'working-class' women were members of trade unions and taking an interest in politics and rights. Many of them were also supporters of the suffragist movement. There's also another misconception that the only people championing 'votes for women' in Britain were the suffragettes, who shouldn't be confused with the suffragists. Suffragists believed in fighting for the cause by peaceful means. Suffragettes had a more **militant** approach. They were prepared to break the law. In fact, they *wanted* to get arrested so as to get in the newspapers and further the cause. Especially as, once in prison, they would often go on hunger strike to gain yet more publicity.

## THE PANKHURSTS

Probably the most famous suffragette was Emmeline Pankhurst. She started out as a suffragist but, frustrated at how peaceful means didn't seem to be getting them anywhere, decided to become a suffragette and take direct action. Such action included women smashing shop windows and street lamps, burning down empty buildings and sports pavilions, slashing paintings in art galleries, pouring acid over golf courses, hassling and heckling politicians, holding marches and public meetings, and generally keeping the issue of votes for women in the public eye. Pankhurst herself was arrested a number of times between 1908 and 1913. When the First World War (1914–18) broke out, many suffragists and suffragettes put the issue of votes for women aside to concentrate on war work.

## EARLY BEGINNINGS

But how did the women's suffrage campaign come to be? One milestone was the publication of *A Vindication of the Rights of Woman* in 1792, by the British writer Mary Wollstonecraft. In it, amongst other things, Wollstonecraft argued for the equality of men and women in everything from education to opportunities. A remarkable person, she spent a number of years in Paris during the French Revolution before finally settling in England. (Her daughter, also called Mary, married the poet Shelley and wrote an even more famous book: *Frankenstein* in 1818.)

Mary Wollstonecraft's *Rights of Woman* became a talking point, and a 'bible' for many early feminists.

## ON THE AGENDA

During the 1830s and 1840s, suffragism really began to gather momentum. The Chartists, who were interested in all aspects of human rights – their name coming from a 'people's charter' submitted to Parliament in 1837 – were supporters of votes for women. It's important to remember that in Britain in those days not all adult men had the vote either. There were a number of requirements a man needed before having that right, and many poor and working-class men were excluded, so women's suffrage could be added to fighting for these men's causes. Suffragists also had the support of men such as John Stuart Mill (an economist and philosopher)  who, in 1865, was one of the co-founders of the first women's suffrage association. The monarch at the time was Queen Victoria but – despite her own authority and responsibilities as a woman – she was totally against the idea of women getting the vote.

## UNITY AND DISSENT

It was in 1897 that the various different women's suffrage groups joined together to form the National Union of Women's Suffrage Societies. It was six years later, in 1903, that Emmeline Pankhurst broke away to form the Women's Social Political Union and its members became the suffragettes. It was almost ten years after that that Emily Davidson stood in front of the king's horse at Epsom Downs and was killed. Then came the war . . .

## THE WAR IS ENDED

In 1918, the year the First World War ended, and partly due to women taking over men's jobs during that war, the

British government gave voting rights to certain women. These were 'women householders, wives of householders and women university graduates over 30'. That still excluded a lot of women, but it was a start and an incredible victory for all those people who had fought for their rights, then put aside their differences to help their country fight for a different cause. In 1928, British women were given the same voting rights as men. The battle had been won.

## MEANWHILE, IN AMERICA . . .

With women excluded from voting the world over, the fight for the right was by no means limited to Britain, and many countries have their own heroes and heroines of the cause. In the US, many women wished to become actively involved in the movement to abolish slavery (see *WOW!*

*Events that Changed the World*) but found that they were made unwelcome by some male campaigners. Many women then set up their own all-women abolitionist societies, but also campaigned to be heard in the more general assemblies. In 1848 the first women's rights convention met in Seneca Falls, New York. There were between 100 and 300 people there, depending on whose reports you choose to believe, but we do know that it was a mixture of both men and women. Public reaction was generally very negative and newspapers tried to ridicule suffragists as being members of a 'shrieking sisterhood'. Many suffragists were physically attacked at public meetings, which were regularly stormed by thugs. Then came the American Civil War.

## AFTER THE WAR

The greatest split between the abolitionists and the suffragists came after the war, in which the American union was saved from splitting up and the slave-owning southern confederacy was defeated. Abolitionists feared that women demanding votes would make it harder for them to gain votes for freed black slaves – in other words, the women's issue was 'getting in the way' of what they saw as the main issue.

## SAME GOAL, DIFFERENT APPROACHES

In 1868, there was a split within the suffragist movement itself, with the setting up of two different associations. The National Woman Suffrage Association was set up to campaign for a federal law, which would cover the whole of the US, granting voting rights to women everywhere in the country at the same time. The American Woman Suffrage Association, set up six months later, however, aimed to get voting rights for women state by state. They argued that if they could at least get votes for women in some states, it would help in the campaign to get votes in others and so on, until women everywhere could vote. This second approach had some early successes. A year later, Wyoming became the first state to give women the vote.

## A CHANGE TO THE CONSTITUTION

Other states followed suit, with Colombia giving women the vote in 1893, Utah and Idaho in 1896, Washington in 1910 and California in 1911, followed by nine others up until 1918. Then in 1919, after the First World War, women in *all* states were granted the vote under the 19th Amendment to the US Constitution. The woman's suffrage amendment had been put before Congress to vote on every year since 1878, thanks to the hard work of Elizabeth Cady Stanton. As well as being the leader of the *National* Woman Suffrage Association, Elizabeth Cady Stanton, along with Susan B. Anthony, is probably one of the most famous name in the American fight for women's rights. Susan B. Anthony, who fought for the cause for 50 years, was the first woman to have her image appear on an American coin. Thanks to the efforts of these and other suffragists, suffragettes and their supporters – both men and women – women now have a voice in democracies the world over. Switzerland was the last European country to give women the vote, but women in several Arab countries still do not have voting rights today. The struggle continues.

# PASSIVE RESISTANCE

## 30 JANUARY 1948, ACROSS INDIA

The prime minister of India, Jawaharlal Nehru, is addressing the Indian people in a radio broadcast, his voice full of emotion. 'Friends and comrades,' he begins, 'the light has gone out of our lives and there is darkness everywhere . . .' He goes on to tell the stunned and grieving audience of listeners that Mahatma Gandhi, known as 'the Father of the Nation', has been assassinated. But Nehru has a warning. No one must seek revenge for what has happened through anger, because 'nothing would displease his soul so much as to see that we have indulged in . . . any violence.' Gandhi had helped win them their independence, only six months ago, through totally peaceful means.

## OUT OF THE ORDINARY

In a world with a history filled with terrible and bloody wars, passive resistance is the unusual idea that oppression can be confronted, and eventually even beaten, by peaceful means. It is based on the principle of what Christians call 'turning the other cheek' – if you're hit on the cheek, don't hit back, but turn the other cheek and offer that one as a target too. The followers of Martin

Luther King Jnr. used passive resistance to fight racism in the US (which you can read about in the next chapter). When white policemen set their dogs and then high-pressure hoses on a march made up of mainly black men, women and children, the marchers didn't fight back. If they had, it'd just have been another running street battle. As it was, the world saw pictures of ruthless white authority figures attacking innocent black people, and the impact was far, far greater.

## NOT A SHOT IN ANGER

Passive resistance can work in many different ways. During the Second World War, Jewish people in countries **occupied** by the Germans were required to wear a yellow star, to be easily identified as Jewish. Not to wear a star could lead to serious trouble. In Denmark, Jewish people followed the instructions but – as a passive act of defiance – a great many non-Jewish people wore the yellow star too.

Now the Germans couldn't tell who was Jewish at a glance. When the time came for Danish Jews to be rounded up and deported to the death camps, they'd all disappeared. The other Danes had taken all 6,000 of them in small boats across the sea to the safety of Sweden. Here was a great victory without a single act of violence.

75

# THE SEEDS OF PEACEFUL RESISTANCE

One of the first people to use the term 'civil disobedience' – a form of passive resistance involving non-cooperation with the authorities (in other words, not doing what the authorities want, but not getting violent about it) – was American Henry Thoreau (1817–62). In 1846, a part of everyone's poll tax (the tax all registered voters had to pay) went towards funding US soldiers in the Mexican War (1846–48). Because Thoreau thought that the whole war was wrong, he didn't want a single cent of his money to go towards funding it, so he refused to pay his poll tax, making it clear why. As a result, he ended up in jail. He laid out his reasons in more detail in a famous essay called *Resistance to Civil Government* in 1849, outlining how passive resistance such as his could be effective under other circumstances too. The world-famous novelist Leon Tolstoy (1828–1910) is also credited with having influenced the passive resistance movement with his writings on the love for all humans and non-violent resistance to 'the forces of evil' as defined in the Bible.

## MEET MAHATMA

The greatest **exponent** of passive resistance was the Indian leader Gandhi (1869–1948) who used non-cooperation and non-violent resistance to British occupation of his country. Mohandas Gandhi, often referred to as Mahatma Gandhi – 'mahatma' means 'great soul' – described himself as a 'soldier of peace'. It's brave enough to take up a weapon and fight for your country. It's even braver to fight for your country without a weapon – especially when the enemy were the well-armed British rulers of India. Gandhi had actually been educated in Britain, and got a law degree at University College, London. Back in India, a firm with business interests in South Africa sent Gandhi there as a representative, and it was there that he developed his ideas on resisting injustice.

## GANDHI IN SOUTH AFRICA

Being a 'non-white' person, he found himself being treated like a second-class citizen. (You can read about South Africa, racism and **apartheid** and its eventual downfall in *Wow! Events that Changed the World*.) Gandhi was horrified by the way that Indians were treated in South Africa and committed his life to improving their plight. After being badly beaten by white South Africans in 1896, Gandhi began suggesting passive resistance and non-cooperation towards the South African authorities, calling his approach 'satyagraha' which, roughly translated, means 'defence of truth by truth'. Gandhi ended up spending over 20 years in South Africa, only leaving once many of the changes he'd so peacefully fought for – such as the South Africans finally accepting Indian marriages as legal – had come into being.

# BRITISH FEARS IN INDIA

Back in his home country of India once more, in 1915, Gandhi now turned his 'satyagraha' on the British **colonial** rulers. He wanted India to rule itself. The British government was worried and, in 1919, the British parliament passed the Rowlatt Acts which gave the colonial rulers extra power to suppress any such 'revolutionary activities', violent or not. In that same year, a demonstration against the acts resulted in a terrible massacre of about 400  peaceful protesters in Amritsar, when soldiers in the British army opened fire on them. A whole series of campaigns of non-cooperation followed between 1920 and 1944, involving millions of Indians – and I don't just mean 'a lot', I really do mean *millions*. Gandhi himself was jailed a number of times. Slowly but surely, he gained attention from and then influence over the British authorities. They realized that his movement of passive resistance wasn't about to go away. Though Britain had experience of crushing armed rebellions, peaceful ones were harder to deal with.

## THE STRUGGLE STRENGTHENS

'Satyagraha' didn't just mean unarmed demonstrators sitting in the street blocking traffic, and not raising an arm against their attackers if hit, spat at or even dragged away. It also meant that Indians resigned from the civil service and all public appointments. Indians wouldn't attend court if summoned, because they didn't recognize its authority. They didn't send their children to government schools. Indians also **boycotted** British goods, and people in the villages began to make more and more of their own. Knowing that many Indians would suffer many hardships when standing up to authority, Gandhi lived a very simple life himself. Not all pro-Independence Indians believed in Gandhi's peaceful approach, however, and a number of violent armed attacks on the colonial British rulers greatly distressed him. For a while, he withdrew from the cause. Finally, India gained independence from Britain in 1947, but only at the expense of it being divided into two independent countries: India (which was mainly Hindu) and Pakistan (which was mainly Muslim). This partition led to riots and it was only when Gandhi threatened to fast – go on hunger strike – until they stopped that peace was restored. Gandhi wanted friendship between religions. He always freely admitted that his beliefs had been influenced not only by his own faith, Hinduism, and by the writings of Tolstoy and Thoreau, but also by Christianity. What mattered to him was that people lived peaceful lives together as people. Tragically, in January 1948, Mohandas Gandhi was assassinated by a Hindu extremist.

## PASSIVE RESISTANCE TODAY

Passive resistance is still an approach used by many pressure groups and protesters today. In Britain, many **eco-warrior** groups protesting about road-building or housing developments destroying woodland or countryside put themselves between the environment and the bulldozers – chaining themselves to blocks of concrete or living up trees and down tunnels to slow the whole process of clearing the land. Another example is of countries boycotting other countries' goods. During white apartheid rule in South Africa, many countries boycotted South African goods. They couldn't directly attack South Africa but, by peaceful means, they could damage the country's economy, trade, power and status in the world. Passive resistance can be very effective in causing world change.

# AMERICAN CIVIL RIGHTS

## 1 DECEMBER 1955, MONTGOMERY, ALABAMA, USA

Rosa Parks is sitting in her seat on the bus. Although both white and black people can travel on the same bus together, the rules are a clear: if a white person wants a seat and you're black, you get right up and give it to him. And that's exactly what Ms Parks is being asked to do – being told to do – day in, day out. But not today. On this particular December morning, Rosa Parks isn't about to give up her seat to anyone. It's going to get her arrested. It's going to lose her her job, but it's also going to be seen by many as the starting point of the modern American civil rights movement – fighting for blacks and whites to be treated equally.

## SEGREGATION

The idea that all people should be treated equally regardless of the colour of their skin seems an obvious one. Anything else is outrageous, but it's an idea that has had to be fought for in the US through the courts, in government and on the streets. Slavery was abolished in the US in the 1860s (and you can read about this in *WOW! Events that Changed the World*) but the fight for black people to be treated the same way as whites – to have the same civil rights – dates back further than that. In the past, the US was a segregated country: black people and white people lived apart, went to separate schools and often couldn't even sit on the same bench. ('Whites Only' signs seemed to be everywhere.)

## DIFFERENT STATES, DIFFERENT LAWS

It's important to remember that, in the US, as well as national laws covering the whole country, states can make their own laws, unique to their own particular state. Segregation laws, therefore, varied from state to state. The laws were often referred to as 'Jim Crow' after a terrible **stereotyped** and unflattering black character from the music hall of the 1830s. (So a person might say that Jim Crow wouldn't let him do something, rather than saying segregation didn't allow it.) The southern states are more famous for their segregation, but the northern states – which fought against slavery and for keeping the states united in the American Civil War (1861–65) – had segregation laws too.

## ROBERTS v. THE CITY OF BOSTON

In 1849, a man named Benjamin Franklin Roberts took the authorities of the city of Boston, in the northern state of Massachusetts, to court to try to force them allow his daughter to go to the local elementary school, nearest to his home. The problem was that Roberts and his daughter were black and the local school was for white children only. He was represented by a black lawyer named Robert Morris and by a white man named Charles Sumner. Franklin Roberts lost his case and his daughter didn't get to go to the school he wanted for her but, just six years later, segregation in all Massachusetts state-run schools was, indeed scrapped. And Charles Sumner, who'd been elected to the US Senate in 1851, went on to write the Civil Rights Act of 1875 – but that's jumping ahead.

## 'NON-CITIZENS'

In 1857, the Supreme Court of the United States declared that a black person couldn't be a US citizen! Before the American Civil War, black people weren't even allowed to be members of the army or navy, either. When the war started, however, many black men joined the **Union** army, in 'all black' units, such as the 4th US Colored Infantry. Despite poorer equipment and, often, less pay than their fellow white soldiers, black soldiers played an important part in the

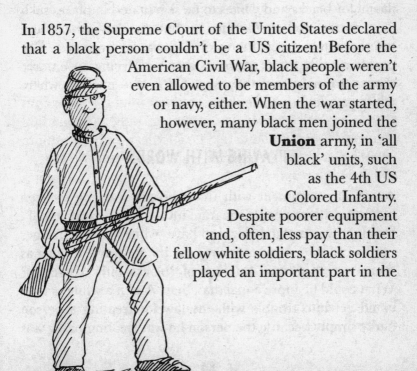

civil war, 23 of them being awarded America's highest award for bravery, the 'Medal of Honor'.

## NEW RIGHTS, OLD PREJUDICES

With the war over, the northern states victorious, and the US still united, three important amendments were made to the United States Constitution. The 13th, 14th and 15th Amendments were made in 1865, 1868 and 1870 and ended slavery, made black people US citizens, with equal protection under the law, and prohibited racial discrimination in voting – black or white, you could vote (if you were a man). Most northern states scrapped segregation altogether. Sumner's Civil Rights Act made it illegal for blacks and whites to be segregated in places such as theatres and restaurants – but the unfairness and discrimination across the whole US was far from over. The problem with these national laws was trying to enforce them – to make sure they were followed – in states where white people didn't like them.

## PLAYING WITH WORDS

A popular argument with those people wanting to keep black and white people separate involved the word 'equal'. Surely it was perfectly legal to have 'whites only' carriages on the railroad – as Americans call the railway – as long as there were an equal number of 'blacks only' carriages? What could be more equal than that? And if a white person could get into trouble with the law for treating a person badly simply because the person he was treating badly was

84

black – and who was to say he might not have treated that same person badly even if he was white? – surely the law wasn't being very equal? Wasn't it favouring blacks over whites? Of course, this false argument completely overlooked that it was always the white people who had the better railway carriages, much more power and were doing the discriminating – but the US Supreme Court regularly agreed with this kind of argument and came down in favour of the segregators!

## DESTROYING OF RIGHTS

Some states used even sneakier methods to try to stop black people voting, typical of which was Mississippi. Once black people had become US citizens and been given voting rights, just under 200,000 of them registered and voted – so the state introduced new rules and regulations for voters in the 1890, to try to stop them. First, anyone who wanted to vote had to pay a regular poll tax, which was far too expensive for most black people, who hadn't long been freed from slavery and were in the lowest paid jobs. Secondly, no one could vote unless they'd passed a reading and writing test. Again, this was deliberately designed to exclude black people because most of those lucky enough to have received an education (and that wasn't all of them by any means) wouldn't have received the same *quality* of education as most white people. The same was happening right across the southern states. Nowhere in the south could a black person marry a white person and, in some states, a black minister wasn't even allowed to perform the marriage ceremony of two white people.

# ORGANIZED MAYHEM

Sadly, things got worse, not better. A society of white terrorists called the Ku Klux Klan – not the *Klu* Klux Klan as people often say – had been formed in the 1860s, which used dreadful violence and threats to keep segregation alive. Members wore white robes and pointed white hoods to cover their heads and hide their identity. Smaller local groups, called Klaverns, grew up and, over the years, many black people were murdered by white people, a common method being 'lynching', when the victim was hanged from a tree. (Over 2,000 were killed that way in fifteen years alone.) Many Klaverns got so out of hand that the Klan disowned them. Then the original Klan itself disbanded in 1871. The modern Klan, which still exists today, was founded in 1915.

## THE NAACP

Those fighting for racial equality, meanwhile, were doing their own organizing. Following a meeting at Niagara Falls, Canada, where blacks and whites discussed ways of fighting for rights, the National Association for the Advancement of Colored People (NAACP) was formed in 1909. It was made up of a mixture of both white and black activists, and they began challenging segregation laws in courts across the land. They successfully overturned a number of laws, opening institutions like law schools as well as sections of the community to blacks as well as whites.

## THE SECOND WORLD WAR

During the 1930s, vast numbers of black people left the more hostile southern states to settle in the more welcoming northern ones. Here, they encountered less racism, and better education and job opportunities. Not only that, in the south in the past, most black Americans had lived in the countryside. Now more and more of them were living and working in towns and cities, in closer proximity to each other, and nearer white people. Because black people could vote in the northern states, and in large numbers, more and more pro-civil rights and anti-segregation politicians were getting elected. Then there was the war itself: membership of the NAACP increased by 1000 per cent, newspapers published by black people for black people campaigned for victory against the fascists abroad and against the racists at home, and black and white soldiers fought alongside each other in huge numbers. Things would never be quite the same again.

## MODERN CIVIL RIGHTS MOVEMENT

Then, on that December day in 1955, Rosa Parks was arrested in Montgomery for failing to give up her seat on the bus. She was an active member of the NAACP, and her branch organized a boycott of the bus service. Almost all the black people in Montgomery stopped using the buses and suddenly the bus company found itself short of about

87

50,000 potential customers! The boycott lasted a year and, in November 1956, a federal law was passed stopping segregation in any form on buses. All passengers should be treated equally.

## MARTIN LUTHER KING JR.

The man who organized the boycott was a black Baptist minister by the name of Martin Luther King Jr. (The 'Jr.' stood for 'Junior' because his father's name was Martin Luther King too.) As well as being a committed Christian and an excellent organizer, he was also an inspiring speaker and soon became a public figure, well-known across America. He wasn't only popular with black people, but also with many white northerners. He arranged rallies, marches and demonstrations but insisted that they always be peaceful. He believed in passive resistance, the idea that violence and force can eventually be defeated by peaceful means – the idea looked at in the previous chapter of this book.

## THE BASIC RIGHTS OF FREEDOM

The modern civil rights movement didn't only want to abolish all traces of segregation, it also called for freedom of speech and freedom of religious beliefs, and for these laws to be protected and enforced by the goodwill of the people in power, not simply be there on the statute book and ignored at state or county level. Based on these beliefs, Martin Luther King Jr. formed special links with Jewish and Protestant groups and his voice of protest for civil rights became louder and louder.

## THE GATHERING MOMENTUM

The 1960s saw a whole variety of protests, from college sit-ins to 'freedom rides' on buses, from state to state, with many ending in violence against the protesters. In 1962, black student James Meredith won a right, through the court, to attend the all-white Mississippi University. The governor of the state, however, was against his attending and tried to stop him enrolling. Finally, President Kennedy had to supply Meredith with a bodyguard of federal marshals so that he could get into the building. Anti-black riots broke out and, along with over 300 people injured, two people actually died. When a similar incident occurred with enrolment in Alabama, in 1963, Kennedy sent in the army! That same year, a key turning point came in Birmingham, Alabama, when pictures of white police officers attacking peaceful black marchers (many of them children) with dogs and water hoses, were shown around the world.

## 'I HAVE A DREAM'

In August 1963, 200,000 supporters of civil rights marched through the US's capital city, Washington, DC. There,

Martin Luther King Jr. gave one of the most famous speeches in US history, which included the words: 'I have a dream that my four little children will one day live in a nation where they will not be judged by the colour of their skin but by the content of their character. I have a dream today!' President Kennedy, who proposed a new Civil Rights Act, was assassinated that November. Tragically, Martin Luther King was also assassinated, but not until 1968, and not until he had achieved much more in the fight for civil rights.

## TODAY

Although one of equality's finest exponents, Martin Luther King Jr. was only one person in a series of groups and individuals who'd been fighting for change, in their own different ways, for over a hundred years. There were, for example, black leaders such as Malcolm X – himself assassinated in 1965 – who believed that equality couldn't be achieved using King's peaceful methods and should be achieved 'by any means necessary'. There are those who would argue that they are still fighting for civil rights in the US today. In April 1992, 58 people were killed and over $750 million of damage was caused in riots in Los Angeles following the **acquittal** of four white police officers. They'd been charged with the severe beating of a black man named Rodney King, and were acquitted despite the whole attack having been recorded on videotape. Even though two officers were later found guilty, many black and white people felt that this was further proof that the battle for civil rights has yet to be fully won. The US has come a long way, however, since Rosa Parks refused to give up her seat on that bus.

# GLOSSARY

**abstract** – without reference to a specific incident. Difficult to understand and relate to everyday existence

**acquittal** – the process of being found 'not guilty' in a trial

**apartheid** – the official South African government policy of dividing and treating people according to the colour of their skin

**baptize** – to duck in or sprinkle a person with water as a sign that they are a member of the Christian Church

**blacklisted** – put on a list of those considered untrustworthy or disloyal, preventing them from working in certain jobs (such as the film industry)

**boycotted** – if people or businesses are boycotted, no one will have dealings with them, buying or selling (Named after a nineteenth-century land agent called Captain Boycott who upset his tenants, and ended up the victim of a boycott!)

**c. –** short for the Latin word 'circa' meaning 'about'. A date marked *c.* means an approximate date; the event occurred around about then

**capitalists** – followers of capitalism, the system whereby goods and production are owned privately, not by the state (as with Communism)

**colonial** – a colonial power was a power which ruled other, separate countries, called colonies. Britain was the colonial power of India. She, and not the Indians, ruled the country

**defect** – to desert your country or state to join one with different, usually opposite, views

**democracy** – a society where the government is ruled by elected representatives of (at least some of) the people

**devout** – deeply religious

**Dowager** – a widow who still holds the title she had from being married to her now-dead husband (Catherine was queen in her own right when married to the king and, when her son became king, she still had the title 'queen')

**eco-warriors** – a nickname for activists who take direct action (usually non-violent) over issues about the environment

**economy** – the management of finances, imports, exports, production, and all in-comings and out-goings of a country

**exile** – living in exile means that you've been forced to live outside your homeland, against your will

**exponent** – someone who upholds an idea or cause

**fasting** – not eating (especially as a part of a religious ritual)

**genes** – a part of DNA, in a fixed position in a chromosome, which determine particular characteristics (e.g. a 'tall' gene or a 'blue eyes' gene)

**Genesis** – The first book in the Old Testament of the Bible, covering the stories of the creation of the Earth, and Adam and Eve in the Garden of Eden

**hysteria** – an uncontrollable emotion (such as panic or fear), or a physical ailment (such as loss of memory) with no 'bodily' cause, it's all in the mind

**incarnation** – a particular form. The god Vishnu is said to have appeared in a number of different forms, or incarnations. Those who believe in reincarnation believe that people come back (after death) in different incarnations too

**independently** – on your own, without help from others

**interest** – money earned on money saved and paid on money borrowed

**lineage** – a line of descendants from an ancestor

**militant** – aggressive and vigorous

**misconceptions** – commonly held beliefs that aren't actually true

**monarch** – a king or queen

**neurologist** – a specialist on the human nervous system

**occupied** – countries occupied by Germany in wartime, for example, were those countries taken over by Germany, against their will

**Protestant** – Protestants are any Christians who aren't Roman Catholics

**reincarnation** – the belief that on death the soul leaves the body and is born again in another body

**republic** – a country or state which doesn't have a king, queen or emperor

**southern hemisphere** – the half of the Earth lying to the south of the Equator (represented by the bottom half of a globe if you slice it horizontally through the middle)

**stereotype** – a typical idea or image of a group of people, often wholly inaccurate (e.g. 'all fat people are lazy')

**sustenance** – nourishment, a way of maintaining health, livelihood and life

**temperate** – moderate or mild

**Union** – Union soldiers were those who fought to keep the states of the USA united in the US civil war, and mostly came from the north. They were fighting Confederacy troops, who wanted to break away to form a separate group of states

**Vedic** – from the earliest religion of the Aryan settlers in India